RANCHING WITH RANDON

WRITTEN BY CHEYENNE CLAXTON

ILLUSTRATED BY JORDAN FINNEY

LifeRich Publishing is a registered trademark of The Reader's Digest Association, Inc.

LifeRich Publishing books may be ordered through booksellers or by contacting:

LifeRich Publishing
1663 Liberty Drive
Bloomington, IN 47403
www.liferichpublishing.com
844-686-9607

ISBN: 978-1-4897-3485-3 (sc)
ISBN: 978-1-4897-3484-6 (hc)
ISBN: 978-1-4897-3486-0 (e)

Print information available on the last page.

LifeRich Publishing rev. date: 04/05/2021

This book is dedicated to my husband, Rex, and son, Randon. Thank you both for teaching me that you're never too old or too young to learn something new. Thank you for inspiring and supporting me to follow through with my dream of writing a book.

Ranch Lesson

No matter where you are or who you are, you can always learn something new!

Hi there! My name is Randon. I live on a ranch in southwest Oklahoma with my mom and dad. We just moved here from Texas!

Every morning I like to dress in my finest cowboy duds, which includes a long-sleeve shirt, denim jeans, cowboy boots, a tooled leather belt, and a cowboy hat. To complete my look, I put on one of my favorite bow ties. It gives me that classic cowboy look. Don't ya think so?

After I'm dressed, I mosey into the kitchen where my mom has whipped up the most scrumdidliumptious breakfast a cowboy could ever ask for. My mom is downright the best cook in all of Cotton County!

Her biscuits are as fluffy as clouds! I like to take a big, fat, juicy piece of sausage and make a good ol' fashioned sausage and biscuit. Oh! And I can't forget to quench my thirst with a glass of cold milk. It does the body good, ya know!

Once my belly is full to the brim, I head to the barn to feed the hungry horses. We have four horses named Sketti, Bubba, Superman, and Cream Puff.

While the horses are munching on their grain, my dad and I will start feeding the cattle. This is one of my favorite things to do! After all the feed is put out, we have to count all of them! One, two, three, four—whoa, there's a lot!

Sometimes there are over one hundred head of cattle in a pasture. Feeding our cattle everyday has taught me to count all the way to one hundred, and I haven't even been to kindergarten yet!

When I feed with my mom, we like to give each one a sweet name because we love desserts! The Herefords are red velvets, the spotted ones are chocolate chips, and the ol' Charolais are buttercreams.

Gee whiz! All this talk of food makes me hungry as a hippo. Good thing lunch is just around the corner!

As soon as lunch is done, I run like a bolt of lightning to the mailbox. You never know what the mail lady is going to deliver. We have the best mail lady in the whole wide world because she not only brings our mail but also leaves candy in the mailbox just for me! She's a real sweetheart!

After I dump the mail on my dad's desk, I like to read the return addresses and sort them into piles. It's kind of like sorting cattle, but the envelopes aren't mooing or trying to run ya over.

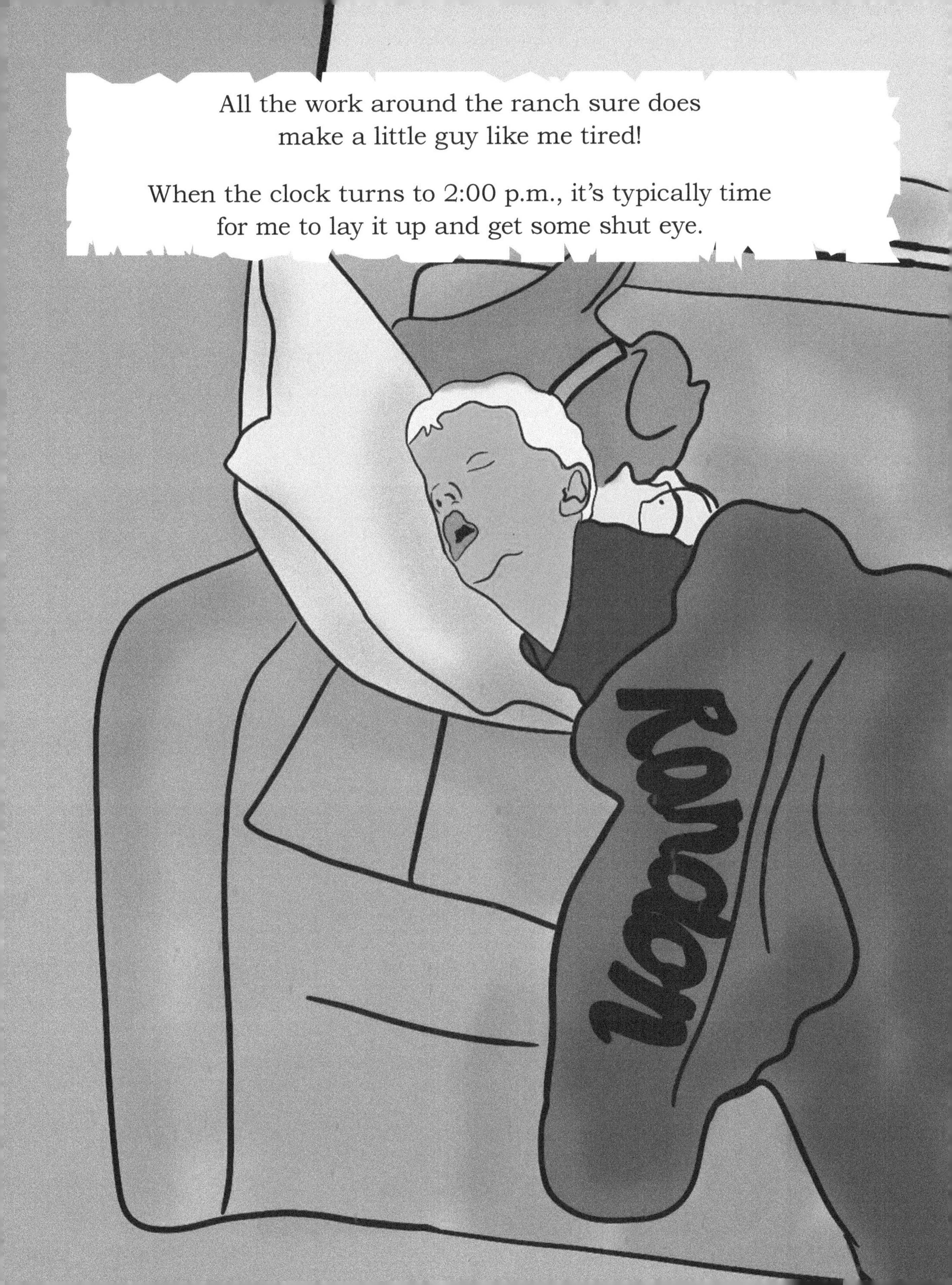

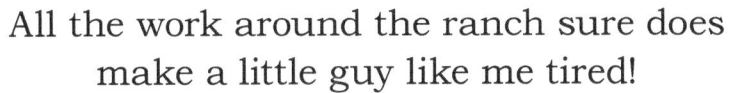

All the work around the ranch sure does
make a little guy like me tired!

When the clock turns to 2:00 p.m., it's typically time
for me to lay it up and get some shut eye.

When I'm done resting, I am refreshed and ready for more ranching duties. Some afternoons there are fences to fix, hay to put out, and cattle to doctor. There are just not enough hours in the day, and the work never ends. But you know that old saying, "Love what you do and never work a day in your life!" That's ranch work!

It sure is fun learning the three *R*s: readin 'riting, and 'rithmitic on our busy ranch. Ranch life is the best life! Every day is always full of adventure!

Just goes to show you, there are always opportunities to learn. We just have to be looking for them!

I sure am glad you tagged along today! I look forward to seeing ya next time on our ranch!

Ranching Vocabulary

grain—A grain-based feed for horses to eat.

head of cattle—The number of cattle you're trying to count. If someone says they see ten head, this means they are looking at ten cattle.

pasture—The land that is made of grass where the cattle live, eat, sleep, and drink water.

yearlings—Cattle that are under two years of age.

Herefords—Cattle with red and white colors on their body.

Charolais—Cattle with a white or cream color on their body.

sorting cattle—Putting cattle into different groups or pastures.

fence to fix—Repairing any parts of a fence that might be broken.

cattle to doctor—Giving medicine to sick cattle to help them feel better and stay healthy.

Coloring Pages

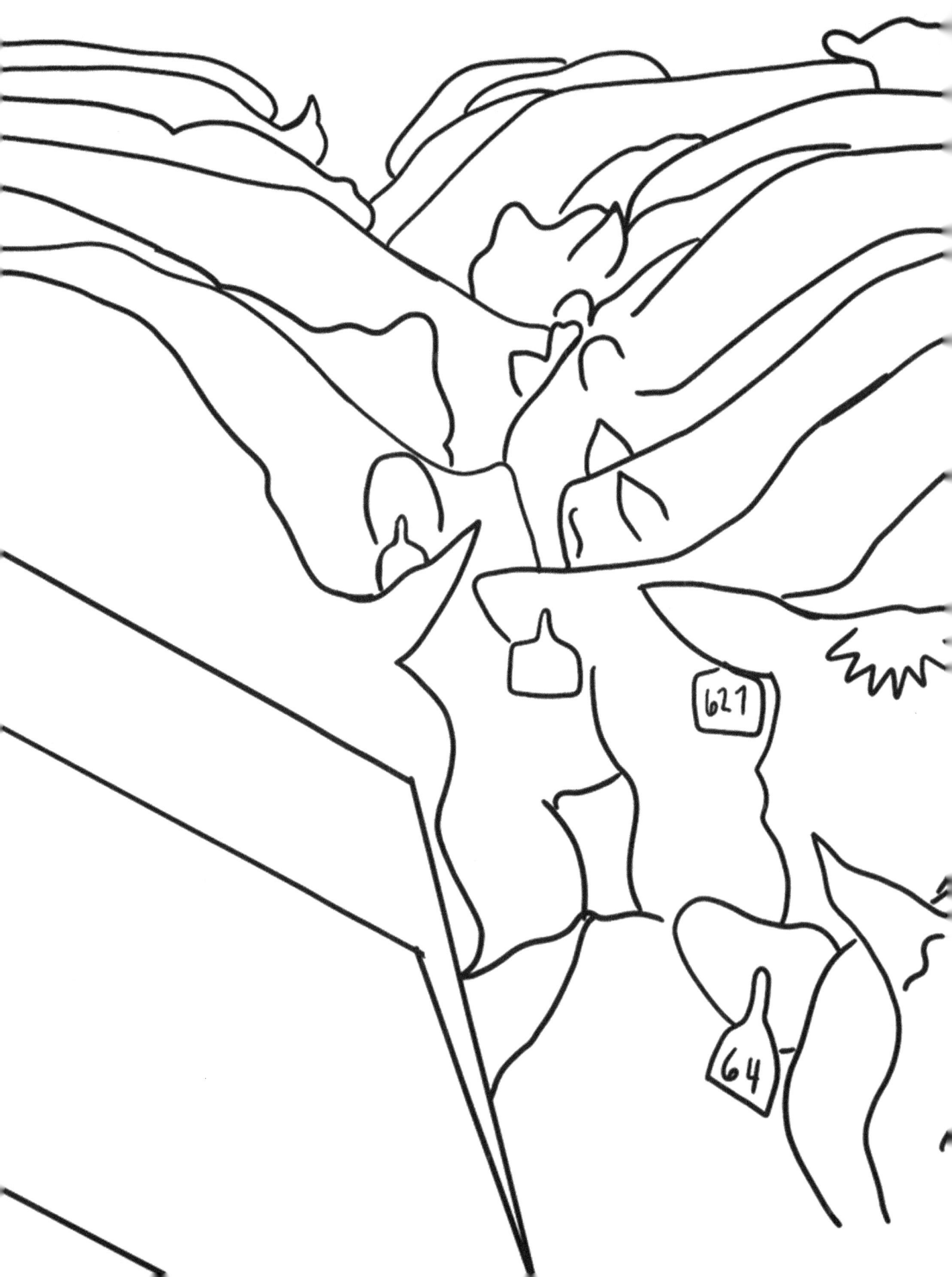

Author Biography

Cheyenne Claxton is a cattleman's wife and cowboy mom. She is a born and raised Texan, but the ranching way of life recently moved her and her family to southwestern Oklahoma. She has always had a love and dream of writing, however she obtained a bachelor's degree in Kinesiology, where she pursued a career as a classroom teacher and girls' athletic coach for 5 years. Cheyenne grew up around the western way of life, as she began competing in rodeo at age 5, and earned countless rodeo accolades in both her high school and collegiate levels of competition. Her time spent as an educator and now as a mom has inspired her to share her love of learning through reading and writing with her first book *"Ranching with Randon"*.

Lightning Source UK Ltd.
Milton Keynes UK
UKHW051018180421
382107UK00002B/91

9 781489 734846